Let's Salute ANDY CAPP

D0711650

Reg Smythe

FAWCETT GOLD MEDAL • NEW YORK

A Fawcett Gold Medal Book
Published by Ballantine Books
Copyright © 1979, 1980 by Daily Newspaper, Ltd.
Distributed by News America Syndicate

Library of Congress Catalog Card Number: 85-90609

ISBN 0-449-12655-2

Manufactured in the United States of America

First Edition: May 1985

10 9 8 7 6 5 4 3 2 1

8-16

WE'RE TOO YOUNG

WE'RE NOT

WE CAN'T AFFORD IT

WE CAN

'OW MUCH DOES IT COST TO GET MARRIED, MISSUS CAPP?

8-16

DUNNO, PET—I'M STILL PAYIN'

8-24

IT'S NOT JUST ME, NONE O' THE OTHER GIRLS AT WORK LIKE 'ER, EITHER...

SHE NEVER OPENS 'ER MOUTH BUT AT SOMEBODY ELSES EXPENSE

I KNOW THE TYPE — SAME AGAIN, PET

'E SHOULD DO — 'E NEVER OPENS 'IS MOUTH BUT AT MY EXPENSE

8-30

9-4

SORRY ABOUT THIS, MISSUS

9-5

IF YOU KNOW OF ANY WAY TO KEEP 'IM OUT OF HOT WATER, APART FROM PUTTIN' DIRTY DISHES INTO IT—

9-7

9-8

9-13

9-27

9-29 Smythe

10-2

10-6

10-11

—AND NOW SHE'S NAGGING ME TO HAVE A PATIO BUILT AT THE BACK, PERCY—

TALK ABOUT KEEPING UP WITH THE JONESES—

AS THOUGH I HAVEN'T ENOUGH ON MY MIND TRYING TO KEEP UP WITH THIS BLOKE!

11-17

12-4

12-5

12-10

HEY, MISTER NOBLE! THANKS FOR HELPIN' FLORRIE 'OME WI' THE SHOPPIN' YESTERDAY, IT MUST 'AVE WEIGHED A TON

GLAD TO HELP, MISTER CAPP

DO YOU SMOKE?

AS A MATTER OF FACT, I DO—

OH, GOOD, I'VE RUN OUT — COULD YOU LEND ME A COUPLE?

12-15

YOU DO MEET SOME FUNNY PEOPLE ....

?

12-20

12-21

A COUPLE OF BILLS —I'LL OPEN THEM IN THE MORNIN'

I SWEAR THAT IF YOU LEAVE TWO BILLS TOGETHER OVERNIGHT, THEY BREED

1-12 Smythe

'E ALWAYS 'AS COMPLETE CONTROL OVER A GAME, BUT NOT OVER 'IMSELF

YOU AN' YOUR MISSUS GET ON VERY WELL TOGETHER, ANDY

ALWAYS 'AVE, ALBERT. IT'S SOMETHIN' WE'VE WORKED OUT BETWEEN US—

1-26

SHE ALWAYS ADMITS WHEN SHE'S IN THE WRONG

YOU, TOO, EH?

THE QUESTION'S NEVER ARISEN

1-30

2-2

RAT-A-TAT!

WHO COULD THAT BE—?

EXCUSE ME, MISSUS CAPP, THERE WAS SUCH A RACKET COMIN' FROM 'ERE LAS' NIGHT— CAN I HELP? WERE YOU HAVIN' A ROW—? OR WAS IT JUST A PARTY—?

SLAM

HALF THE WORLD DOESN'T KNOW 'OW THE OTHER HALF EXISTS—AN' IT'S NONE OF THEIR FLIPPIN' BUSINESS!

2-6

Smythe

2-7 Smythe

3-17

GOOD GAME, PET?

MUCH OF A CROWD?

—PET?

IF YOU *MUST* KNOW — WE GOT THRASHED AGAIN AN' THE CROWD WORE A FAWN COLOURED RAINCOAT

3-20

3-25

ABOUT THE AUTHOR

Reginald Smythe was born in West Hartlepool, England, a town that inspired his cartoon strip, ANDY CAPP—along with his snooker-playing father and Florrie, his mother. Unlike Andy, Reg wanted to work but had a hard time finding a good job, due to the economic depression of the 30's. He went on the dole and unwittingly picked up the material he would later use in his cartoons.

ANDY CAPP first appeared in London's *Daily Mirror* newspaper in 1958. Editors in Europe bought the strip even before it became a national feature in Britain the following year. It seemed the little man with the big fists had universal appeal. He now appears in forty-nine countries, in thirteen languages, and is followed every morning in one thousand different newspapers in the United States. In France he's known as ANDRE CHAPEAU, and in Italy as ANGELO CAPELLO, but fans write to Reginald Smythe saying that Andy has put his finger on the human condition everywhere.

Says Reg: "He may be a horrible little man—but he's been very good to me."